TO WHOM IT MAY CONCERN

By Aurin Squire

To Whom It May Concern was first produced in the 2006 Fresh Fruit Festival in New York City at the Abingdon Theatre. Carol Polcovar, Artistic Director of Fresh Fruit Festival. The production was directed by Erick Herrscher and won festival awards for Best Play, Best Writing, and Best Actor (Ted Caine). The cast was as follows:

LORENZO LAFARHOFF: Ted Caine

MAURICE CREELY: Vincent Ingrisano

To Whom It May Concern received a second production at Arclight Theatre in New York City on March 2008. The production was directed by David Gaard. The cast was as follows:

LORENZO LAFARHOFF: Israel Gutierrez

MAURICE CREELY: Matthew Alford

CHARACTERS
1. Lorenzo Lafarhoff – 15-year-old rural boy
2. Maurice Creely – 20-year-old soldier

TIME

The play takes place in the time period of America's invasion of Afghanistan, roughly between 2003-2015.

STORY

To Whom It May Concern is an epistolary play about transcendent and oft-kilter ways of love and internet relationships. When a 15- year-old boy writes a letter to a soldier and is confused for an older woman, a series of seductive exchanges begins.

NOTES ON STAGING

The play can be staged in a variety of flexible and creative ways. When characters write letters, e-mails or instant messages, the act should be performed with fluidity. Direct address to the audience is probably the smoothest way, but most certainly not the only way. That said, miming the writing or texting without a prop in hand is not preferable. During heightened scenes or to emphasize certain moments, these suggestions can be modified or ignored as seen fit. For instant messaging, the characters can speak out the abbreviations and symbols. Emoticons are printed in bold.

TO WHOM IT MAY CONCERN

SCENE ONE: FIRST LETTER

(Abilene, Kansas and Kabul, Afghanistan.

LORENZO LAFARHOFF, 15, sits in his bedroom writing a letter.

MAURICE A. CREELY, a 20-year-old with glasses, eats cookies and reads the letter.)

LORENZO: To Whom It May Concern at the 1st Marine Division of the United States Armed Forces, I read an article in the Abilene Chronicle and wished to contact Sgt. Maurice A. Creely. I found his rescue story very cool. And I'm not going to lie: I also liked the picture attached to it. I guess you can say this is a fan letter. I'm a student at Carter High School in Abilene, Kansas. I've enclosed a sealed batch of chocolate oatmeal cookies. Hopefully, you can get them to Sgt. Creely before they rot. The army might have a strict policy on packages, but I'd really like to get this to him. Let me know. I have his picture hanging by my bed.

Yours truly,

LL

To Whom It May Concern
© Aurin Squire
Trade Edition, 2015
ISBN 978-1-63092-077-7

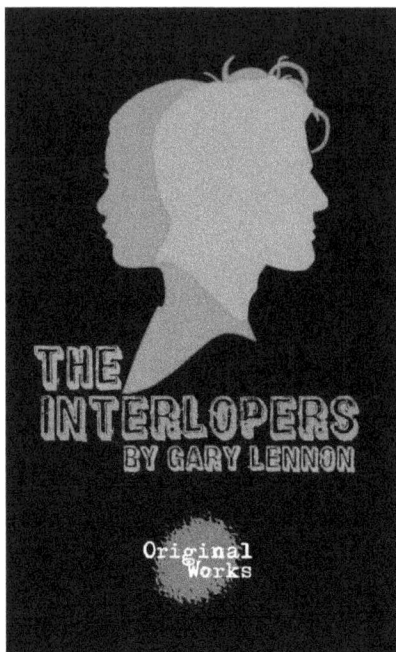

The Interlopers by Gary Lennon

Synopsis: *The Interlopers* is a *Romeo and Juliet* story set in the transgender world of Los Angeles. Through the theme of identity, the play explores a group of unique misfits who call themselves family, and who are brave enough to challenge the obstacle course called life. Examining these singular and special people, the play follows them on their journeys to being their whole and authentic selves.

Cast Size: 6 Males, 2 Females

MAURICE: Dear LL, It is always nice to get a fan letter, especially from a young woman who sounds as sweet as you. And just so you know the army may have a strict policy on receiving packages but I wouldn't know because I'm not in the army. I'm in the Marines. There is a difference. But...no big deal, just an FYI. Anyway, thank you for the cookies. They were delicious. I bet you are too. Ha ha. But seriously. The desert is hot and there are so many bugs it is disgusting. I try not to think about it. Instead I try to picture pretty things. In fact I'm trying to get a picture of you in my head. Do you have one? I would like to see it. I bet you are really...cute. By the way, are you going to be 18 any time soon?

Sincerely,

Maurice Creely

LORENZO: Dear Sgt. Creely, you seem to be under some misconception about me. Perhaps it is my fault. I was hoping that you might be...your sensitivity led me to believe that there was a slight –not great but miniscule- chance that you would be interested in me. I realize you might never want to speak to me again but I can't lie...

(Beat)

LORENZO: I'm one hot teenage girl. I'm 17, so I guess I'm not a girl, not yet a woman. But I will be. Any day now I will blossom into a beautiful young

7

woman. My buds are ripening as I write. Post me back. Please.

Sincerely,

LL… Lillian.

MAURICE: Dear Lillian, I don't know why you would think I would want to stop receiving your letters. Besides your cooking is so delicious I think my entire unit would kill me if I stopped talking to you. I've been telling them all about you and they agree: you are one special almost-legal teenager. I mean, who bakes stuff and mails them to Marines they don't even know? No one. Who takes the time to pick out a lonely…lone face in a crowd and write them a letter? No one even cares about the thousands getting killed. I thought everybody had forgotten about us out here. Your letters give me hope that maybe that's not true. I know I see you, Lillian. And I want to continue seeing you. Especially when you…turn 18. Ha-ha-ha. But seriously: don't stop writing. Yours are the only letters I get. I want to know everything about you. And a picture would be nice, too. I don't know if you have a computer or not, but we should e-mail each other. It'd be a lot quicker way of getting to know each other…

(LORENZO and MAURICE move to computers.)

LORENZO: … I get all wet and moist inside and slip my fingers between my…

(LORENZO flips through an anatomy book and cringes.)

LORENZO: ...labia majora. It feels so good when I rub my...vestibule and clitoris. My vulva gets all tingly and then I explode, shuddering and biting down into my pillow hard. Then I melt like a little kitten, falling asleep thinking about how good you make me feel.

(Beat)

MAURICE: Thank you for the e-mail.

LORENZO: You're welcome. This is a lot quicker than writing. This past month has been so good.

MAURICE: Lillian, I can't stand looking at pictures anymore. When are you going video chat?

LORENZO: I prefer you see me. I've left a ladder by my window just for you. I have to go meet...a friend at the bus stop. For now, I've sent you another sweet treat.

MAURICE: *(taking out her panties)* Thank you for the latest treat. I don't think I'll be sharing this dessert with the unit. Do you have some way we could talk more directly, like instant messaging?

(They switch to instant messaging.)

MAURICE: So good to finally meet you in cyberspace **(smiley face)**.

LORENZO: **(smiley face)** likewise. Btw, if you ever want to talk always here at my computer around this time…after cheerleading practice.

MAURICE: Cheerleading practice? BFG.

LORENZO: What's that?

MAURICE: Big fucking grin.

LORENZO: Well AAP, A3: always a pleasure. Anytime, anyplace, anywhere. Have to leave in a minute but Maurice, u know what I'd do 2 u if you were here. I'd like to…

MAURICE: Oh, now, DEGT. Don't even go there! *(out of the side of his mouth)* Lieutenant is looking over my shoulder and I think he knows about our cyber-love. Don't want 2 make him jealous. I think he likes me.

LORENZO: What?

MAURICE: I think he's a H-O-M-O.

LORENZO: Really?

MAURICE: I know. CYBI: can u believe it?

LORENZO: ICB: I can. Is he cute?

MAURICE: What? You're funny.

LORENZO: Ha-ha, I know. But seriously...would you describe him as...

MAURICE: I don't know. Yeah, I guess he could be considered that. But I'm more interested in seeing a picture of you.

LORENZO: Soon enough. But let's get back 2 this lieutenant.

MAURICE: Come on, Lil...

LORENZO: Don't be shy, this is interesting to me. Is this the same lieutenant as the 1 in the article w/ u?

MAURICE: Yeah.

LORENZO: Maybe he just admires u.

MAURICE: He's got no reason 2.

LORENZO: Course he does. You did something very brave.

MAURICE: That was weeks ago.

LORENZO: Once a hero, always a hero.

MAURICE: U think I'm a hero?

LORENZO: You're a total bad-ass.

MAURICE: Don't really see myself as that sort of guy.

LORENZO: Try seeing yourself differently.

MAURICE: Who am I trying for?

LORENZO: 4 me.

MAURICE: …okay. 4 U I'd do it. So how about giving ur hero some video play?

LORENZO: U really want 1?

MAURICE: Yes! Hop to it, woman.

LORENZO: Yessir. I guess you'll eventually have to see me.

MAURICE: No time like the present.

LORENZO: BRB.

(LORENZO grabs his digital camera and takes a few pictures.)

LORENZO: Gonna send u a pic first.

MAURICE: What? I thought u were-

LORENZO: It's a pic of my friend. Tell me what u think.

MAURICE: -No, Lil.

LORENZO: HOAS.

MAURICE: What?

LORENZO: Hold on a second.

MAURICE: Wow, ur text vocab is huge.

LORENZO: Well I use it a lot. I can talk entirely in acronyms and emojis if I want to. Tell me what u think of this guy?

MAURICE: Lillian, the only picture I want 2 see is yours.

LORENZO: In a second. Maurice, if this lieutenant is H-O-M-O would that be such a bad thing?

MAURICE: No.

LORENZO: Good.

MAURICE: I just don't want those people around me.

LORENZO: PXT, please explain that.

MAURICE: They stay in their place and I can stay in mine.

LORENZO: And what is their place?

MAURICE: Away from me.

LORENZO: Look, I know you guys have this big macho image to uphold being in the army-

MAURICE: -Marines.

LORENZO: -right, whatever but-

MAURICE: -no, baby. It's not whatever. You've done this a few times in our conversation and I've let it slide. Because I like u.

LORENZO: Fine, but-

MAURICE: -there is a big difference. Look: labels are very important. What we call ourselves. What we call others, what we say we believe in. It's very much not a 'whatever' thing. If a guys says he's in the Navy and u keep calling him Coast Guard Bill, he's going 2 get upset. Because he had to earn that label.

LORENZO: Ok, well what if they was born w/ it? Let's say Bill was born into the Navy. Even though he didn't necessarily want to be in it, he was labeled as a seaman.

MAURICE: LOL, **(smiley face)** U said seaman.

LORENZO: **(smiley face)** Anyway he was born w/ a label and expected to spend his whole life at sea. Let's say this person wanted to be on solid ground. In the Marines.

MAURICE: Now ur talking. Well, I'd tell him 2 go sign up.

LORENZO: But what if he couldn't do it, Maurice. What if he couldn't just sign up?

MAURICE: Why not?

LORENZO: Because. He couldn't be on dry land.

MAURICE: Are you talking about somebody like Aquaman? Or something like that?

LORENZO: *(sighing)* OMG...sure. Like Aquaman.

MAURICE: So...Aquaman is in the Navy...

LORENZO: Or something.

MAURICE: But he wants 2B in the Marines? PXT, because I'm confused, I think ur mixing ur analogies.

LORENZO: He wants 2B on land. His family lives on land. They don't understand why he can't come in from sea. They think he's sick, so they send him to a doctor. And when he refuses to get better, when he can't get better, they don't want him any more. They think he's disgusting, b/c of the label he was born with. When he tries to explain they scream. When he tries to touch them, to hug them, they beat him. But they don't understand he would change if he could. Because it's lonely out there.

MAURICE: Can't he find other sea creatures?

LORENZO: None his age. Most of them are hiding. And the creatures he bumps into out there are old and mean. Their skin is wrinkled like prunes and they don't care about him. They've been alone in the ocean for so long that they've forgotten how 2 treat each other. And I...he knows that he's going to become like them. If he doesn't find a way 2 get 2 land or another creature as kind and caring as him, he's going 2B lost at sea. And he doesn't want that cu then he really will be corrupted.

MAURICE: This creature could always...kill himself.

LORENZO: What?

MAURICE: If they are doomed 2B unhappy their whole life why not spare themselves? Why die a thousand deaths when you can die 1?

(Beat)

MAURICE: We're still talking about sea creatures, right?

(Beat)

MAURICE: LL?

LORENZO: IGR.

MAURICE: What?

LORENZO: I gotta run. Meeting a friend in the park.

16

MAURICE: Lillian, who are all these friends UR meeting in parks? And why can't they just come back to UR house? Wait, are U trying to make me jealous?

(LORENZO puts condoms and lotion in a backpack.)

MAURICE: Lillian.

LORENZO: Maybe we shouldn't speak 2 each other 4 a while.

MAURICE: Cuz why?

LORENZO: Cuz I don't feel like talking to U.

MAURICE: Cuz why?

LORENZO: Cuz you're not the sensitive person I thought U were.

MAURICE: Wait. What just happened? Did I do something? If so, I can make it up to U. I sent U a package yesterday.

LORENZO: GFY.

MAURICE: What?

LORENZO: Go. Fuck. Yourself.

MAURICE: LL?

LORENZO: Army brat.

MAURICE: That's not even correct terminology.

LORENZO: Then how bout army boy? Or how bout closeted army faggot.

MAURICE: What?

LORENZO: U heard me, army fag.

MAURICE: Lillian they monitor our computers.

LORENZO: Good, then they'll know that UR an army fag. Maybe U and the lieutenant can

MAURICE: -hey, fuck U, bitch.

LORENZO: -yeah, fuck me and fuck U. Guess we finally agreed on something.

MAURICE: But Lillian, what's going on? Whatever it is, it can be worked out. UR the only...please. I need to speak to U. What am I supposed to do?

LORENZO: Well, I guess U should take UR own advice.

MAURICE: And what's that?

LORENZO: Kill yourself.

SCENE TWO: STORM

(MAURICE walks in with shawl around his head. A sandstorm rages outside while in Kansas, a thunderstorm is passing overhead. MAURICE sits down on his bed and unwraps his shawl.)

MAURICE: Lillian? U there?

(Beat)

MAURICE: U said U were normally online at around this time so I thought I would try. I got an internet hook up to my personal computer by my bed. So we can say whatever we want now. There's a sandstorm outside. All operations have been grounded. Not even the suicide bombers are out today. You can't see your own hands. You ever been in a sandstorm? The air becomes this ocean of yellow and it feels like a hundred glass needles are sticking every inch of your body. On your nose, on your toes, in your eyes all these tiny needles. And every time you breathe, you inhale these needles and it burns your chest and head. You sweat and sand clumps together and runs down your face in little streams. I got all these rivers of dirt and sand running down my arms and chest. I feel like I'm being buried alive.

(Beat)

MAURICE: Look, I'm sorry. I thought about what I said. No one should be ashamed of who they r or label. I really like you and we have nothing to be ashamed of.

So there, r u happy: I don't think Aquaman should kill himself.

(LORENZO enters, with ripped clothes and dripping wet. He's searching under the bed for something.)

MAURICE: If you're there…TMB. That's text me back. I've been chatting and increasing my txt message vocab. I'm sure I'm not at your level yet. I mean that in a lot of ways. Well, I guess you're not there. WWYC. Write When You Can.

LORENZO: Maurice, hey. LTNS.

MAURICE: Long Time No See back at you. How are you?

LORENZO: Wet. Incredibly wet.

MAURICE: **(smiley face, wink, wink)**

LORENZO: Not like that, perv. Came in from a storm.

MAURICE: Me 2.

LORENZO: It's raining over there?

MAURICE: Sandstorm.

LORENZO: What's that like?

MAURICE: *(sarcastic)* Fun.

LORENZO: Wish you were here.

MAURICE: I wish I was there 2.

LORENZO: Your family must miss u.

MAURICE: Don't know.

LORENZO: Y not?

MAURICE: They got their own lives. Hey, wanna cyber-sex, **(smiley face wink)**?

LORENZO: … **(frown)** Not really.

MAURICE: Come on, it'll be fun.

LORENZO: Not in the mood, dude.

MAURICE: Lil, is this about last time? Look, I'm sorry about what I said.

LORENZO: It's not you. Daddy issues.

MAURICE: Ahhh, family crap. Feel your pain.

LORENZO: U2?

MAURICE: 1 of the reasons I joined the Marines.

LORENZO: Really? What about ur Mom?

MAURICE: Gone.

LORENZO: What?

MAURICE: Left when I was in high school.

LORENZO: That's fucked up.

MAURICE: You get used to fucked up things.

LORENZO: Brothers and sister?

MAURICE: 1 Gone. Don't ask.

LORENZO: What happened?

MAURICE: What did I just say?

LORENZO: Sorry…brother or sister?

MAURICE: You really don't know how to follow orders.

LORENZO: Yeah, one of my problems. So…

MAURICE: Brother. Younger. Dead.

LORENZO: Sorry. Dad?

MAURICE: Wish he was dead.

LORENZO: Same here. Maybe. I like my mom better.

MAURICE: Same.

LORENZO: So why did yours leave?

MAURICE: Never said. Guess she just got tired. Woke up one morning. Drank some coffee and walked out.

LORENZO: Creepy. I thought only Dads did shit like that.

MAURICE: Everybody leaves. Eventually. Only fucked up thing is she left the water on in the tub. It was like it was raining in my room. Water was running down the stairs. It took two weeks to dry out everything. And then the mold. On the ceilings, inside the walls, everything stank. Her clothes and stuff were all on her closet floor and they got covered with these green moldy spores.

LORENZO: So she didn't take anything?

MAURICE: 1 thing. It was coming up on a year since my brother was buried. We had a picture of him on a mantel piece that she took that.

LORENZO: What a jerk.

MAURICE: Hey! That's my mother.

LORENZO: Sorry. But it's true.

MAURICE: ...yeah.

LORENZO: If anybody ever did that to me I'd fucking hunt them down.

MAURICE: No, u wouldn't.

LORENZO: I'd hunt them down and, and... blow their fucking brains out.

MAURICE: No, u wouldn't, Lillian. Your too sweet and nice.

LORENZO: Maurice, I'm not that nice.

LORENZO: Maurice, I'm not that nice.

MAURICE: Yeah, u r. That's why u can forgive me so easily.

LORENZO: I haven't forgiven u yet.

MAURICE: But u will.

LORENZO: And how do u know?

MAURICE: Cuz. I'm ur bad-ass hero.

LORENZO: Oh really?

MAURICE: Yeah...I mean, if u want me 2 B.

LORENZO: Maurice, that's not the way a bad-ass hero talks.

MAURICE: I'm in training. I've been working on be-ing...better. B/c of u. I'm trying 2 improve myself, for u. Trying 2 change.

LORENZO: But why? But u haven't even met me.

MAURICE: I think we've met each other. In some way. And I want to be smarter, funnier, and just...more for you.

LORENZO: Don't be more. I'm sorry 4 being so shitty. I hope u can forgive me.

MAURICE: Always. U know, I've never been 2 Kansas.

LORENZO: Not missing much. Can't wait 2 get out of this fucking city. This state. The douchebag heartland of America. Pickup trucks, belt buckles, fried chicken and fat-ass retards with their fat-ass wives and their fat-ass greasy kids.

MAURICE: Is something wrong today?

LORENZO: Just venting. Maybe I could go 2 Kabul.

MAURICE: LOL. Are u serious?

LORENZO: Y not? I can get work. And they can't be setting off bombs on every corner. And I'll wear one of those burkhas. Nobody will see my face or know my name. Just you and me.

MAURICE: Lillian, it's just sand and caves. Can't even understand how these people have been living out here. There's no atmosphere.

LORENZO: That sounds nice.

MAURICE: During the day it's an oven and then at night it's a freezer.

LORENZO: Just want to get out of this town.

MAURICE: You feel like an outsider? Like that Aquaman?

LORENZO: LOL, I guess.

MAURICE: Lillian, it will pass. When I was younger-

LORENZO: -aren't u only 19? I mean u still can't order wine.

MAURICE: 20, and don't interrupt ur elders.

LORENZO: Sorry.

MAURICE: The point is that I felt exactly like U2.

LORENZO: And what did u do about it?

MAURICE: Joined the Marines.

LORENZO: Then I guess it worked out 4 U. UR name is in the paper, U won some medals and now UR a hero.

MAURICE: Yeah, listen Lil. I'm not a bad-ass hero.

LORENZO: Not yet. But U got UR learner's permit.

MAURICE: No, I'm serious.

LORENZO: If I did anything even slightly cool I'd brag 2 everybody.

MAURICE: It's just pure chance who gets in the newspaper. That's all it was. LL, don't join the Marines. Being on dry land isn't what it's cracked up to be. Stay out at sea.

LORENZO: W/ who?

MAURICE: Have some time off soon. Going home to St. Louis. I could take a bus out 2 Kansas.

LORENZO: Ummm…don't inconvenience yourself.

MAURICE: No inconvenience. What else do I have 2 do?

LORENZO: U got friends u want 2 visit?

MAURICE: A few.

LORENZO: Sure u gotta bunch of girls hanging around.

MAURICE: Lillian, my life is a really bad country Western song. My dog died. My mom left. U R it. My only contact w/ someone real. This is for real. At least that's what I think. Don't know how U feel.

LORENZO: Yeah. It's real.

MAURICE: So when I get there…if I get there…I'll finally get 2 CU.

LORENZO: Well, let's talk about that later. We gotta plan it out. Gotta know so I can get myself ready.

MAURICE: What does a young, hot woman like urself have 2 prepare? U gotta fix UR face?

LORENZO: Among other things.

MAURICE: You're just being shy.

LORENZO: Actually I have finals around that time. Studying and preparing to go to college. Don't want you to come all the way out here and be disappointed. Wouldn't want you wasting your time on me.

MAURICE: It wouldn't be a waste **(smiley face)**.

LORENZO: **(smiley face)** I'm sorry 4 telling U2 GFY.

MAURICE: I was more offended by the army reference.

MAURICE: And I'm sorry 4 what I said. Aquaman should live. And all his descendants.

LORENZO: So now we've made up.

MAURICE: Almost. We still have 1 thing 2 do. **(smiley face, wink wink)**

LORENZO: I thought U couldn't because they monitored UR computer.

MAURICE: Everyone sexts. U get the package I sent?

LORENZO: *(taking out jock strap)* Yes, thank u. I sleep w/ every night.

MAURICE: Whaddya do w/?

LORENZO: Rub it.

MAURICE: Where?

LORENZO: On my vulva.

MAURICE: LL...could you...

LORENZO: What is it, MAC68?

MAURICE: When you talk about 'stuff,' be a little less clinical.

LORENZO: LOL. Okay, Big Mo. I take your hot, sweaty jock strap and I rub it on my...vagina.

MAURICE: A little bit better...what else...

LORENZO: And then I let it slide down my, my...pussy lips...

MAURICE: Now you're talking! That's it LL, what else do you do?

LORENZO: Uh-uh, not so fast, cowboy. First tell me what you do with my package?

MAURICE :…let it slide all up and down my…bod. Across my 6-pac abs, and over my pulsating pecs, between my hairy thighs…

LORENZO: Yes, yes…

MAURICE: …then I wrap it around…my .45 magnum.

LORENZO: Yeah, I do the same.

MAURICE: …?

LORENZO: LOL, jk, joking. I mean I press it into my moist, sweet…vulva

MAURICE: **(frown)** Lil-

LORENZO: -cunt. I meant my slick hawt quivering cunt. I press ur jock n2 my sweet warm. And I see u, sneaking n2 my bed. Real quiet like a panther ready 2 pounce on me.

MAURICE: And u under me…

LORENZO: And I'm rolling…

MAURICE: And writhing. Grinding, sweaty and hot…

LORENZO: …pounding me, harder and harder…

MAURICE: You're so sweet, and soft, and gentle. I kiss ur breast and neck as I'm inside. You arch ur back like a cat, oh yes, tell me ur 18...tell me you've turned 18...yes! Oh, I'm coming, I'm coming... *(he exhales in a long sigh)*...XOXO

LORENZO: ...me feeling on ur chest, rubbing my hands across ur hair, down ur stomach, I can feel u inside me, hot. All muscle and sand, gritty and sweating. I'm 18, I'm legal, I'm legal!!! Oh, I'm coming... *(he exhales)* Nighty nite. TTYL, XOXO

MAURICE: LL? Lillian? I can't wait any longer.

SCENE THREE: CREEP

(LORENZO is asleep. MAURICE opens the window and climbs in. He places his bag on the floor and begins taking off his clothes.)

MAURICE: Here I am, Lil. Your desert soldier in the night. Sorry it took so long to get here. Getting extended leave is a bitch. But now that I'm here, I'm going to do it just like we talked about. I even got a blindfold from a NAVY SEAL, you know, if you want to make it more mysterious.

(LORENZO moans and shifts under the covers. MAURICE crawls into bed and rolls the covers over their heads.)

MAURICE: Here I am, Lil. Whew! You kinda big…but that's all right…now turn around and let me get a look at those big brown eyes…

(MAURICE explodes out of the bed.)

MAURICE: Wait, wait…listen, kid. I'm sorry. I thought…I mean…

LORENZO: Please don't hurt me.

MAURICE: No, no, I'm not-

LORENZO: -I won't make a sound. Just take whatever you want.

MAURICE: I climbed in the wrong window.

LORENZO: What?

MAURICE: Be calm. I'm looking for Lillian Lafarhoff.

LORENZO: Huh?

MAURICE: Kid, I'm her...friend. And I was just looking to play a...joke...

LORENZO: Maurice.

(LORENZO turns on the light.)

MAURICE: Yes, that's my name, kid. Just don't call the cops.

LORENZO: You had a look in your eyes like one of those tweaking meth heads who forgets where he is and chops up a whole family while they sleep in their beds like this story I just read about it. Saw about it. One of those news clips online, so I say read when I actually mean watching online. But you're not a crazy meth head who's gonna chop me up so it's cool.

MAURICE: Wait...how do you know my name? (*Door closing off-stage.*)

LORENZO: Hide.

MAURICE: What?

33

LORENZO: I just heard my parent's door open down the hall.

(LORENZO throws the covers over him. LORENZO opens the door and light from the hallway comes in. After a moment, the light goes out. LORENZO locks the door.)

MAURICE: Safe to come out?

LORENZO: Is it ever?

MAURICE: What?

LORENZO: I said just a second. Dad just...walking back from the bathroom.

(He grabs MAURICE's gift jock strap and shoves it under the bed. MAURICE uncovers himself.)

LORENZO: Hi, I'm Lorenzo.

MAURICE: I'm Maurice...but you already know that.

LORENZO: Yeah.

MAURICE: How do you know that?

LORENZO: Because. I'm Lillian's younger brother. She's spoken of you as a...friend.

MAURICE Yes, me and her are just good friends.

(MAURICE becomes aware that he isn't wearing pants. He puts them on. LORENZO grabs a robe for himself.)

MAURICE: I was just…playing a practical joke on her by sneaking up here. Thought her bedroom was here.

LORENZO: Huh?

MAURICE: The window was open.

LORENZO: I like to sleep that way sometimes.

MAURICE: Right. Well…that was pretty funny.

LORENZO: Yeah…

MAURICE: I mean we almost…

LORENZO: *(depressed)* …if it had only been a little bit darker.

MAURICE: Yeah, and you've got really smooth skin.

LORENZO: Thanks.

MAURICE: OH! Not that I'm…I mean, it's just an observation.

LORENZO: I use three different types of acne medication. I've got the bar, the cream, and I make my own facial scrub. Twice a day. You really like my skin?

MAURICE: It was just an observation…it's soft…like a woman. Is Lillian home?

LORENZO: Is Lillian home?

MAURICE: Your sister.

LORENZO: Yes, my sister. She should be home in a little bit.

MAURICE: Isn't it kind of late for her to be out?

LORENZO: Isn't it kind of late? Yes.

MAURICE: Why do you keep repeating what I say?

LORENZO: Why do I keep...I'm joking. It's a nervous habit when I'm trying to think of something to say. Otherwise if I don't, I just...

(LORENZO stares at him for a long time.)

LORENZO: And that's when people get nervous, like you just did. So I figured it's better to just keep shoveling coal into the ol' furnace. Even when the train isn't going anywhere. Keep the pistons pumping, the jets blazing, the feet jogging.

MAURICE: What is your sister doing out so late?

LORENZO: Cheerleading practice.

MAURICE At 11:30 at night?

LORENZO: After practice she hangs out with the cheersluts. She's really dedicated. I told her that it's just cheerleading but she was like all, 'shut up. I love to cheer. Yay!' But I guess it's worth it when you

36

look at her *(looking at him)* taut, lean muscular body. You should wait here until she comes home. We can hang out.

MAURICE: I've got a bus back to St. Louis in the morning. I can go away and then come back before then.

LORENZO: No, that's too much trouble for you. And she really wants to see you, Please don't go. She would be so disappointed.

MAURICE: I can't wait all night.

LORENZO: Of course.

MAURICE: A few minutes. So…is it Lorenzo?

LORENZO: Sure. Whatever you want.

(LORENZO dims the lights.)

MAURICE: Why did you just do that?

LORENZO: The lights hurt my eyes. I just woke up.

MAURICE: Right. So, Lorenzo…

(LORENZO hits the play button on his laptop and rock blasts. He quickly switches it off.)

MAURICE Should I hide again?

LORENZO: No, it's fine. I hit the wrong button.

MAURICE: He can't come in here, right?

LORENZO: Nope. Door is locked. And they're down the hall anyway. We only have to worry if you hear the door opening for a bathroom run. My Dad wakes up a lot. Big man. Tiny bladder.

MAURICE: That sucks.

LORENZO: If he lost some weight his belly blubber wouldn't crush his tiny bladder. But he loves the Ham & Eggery. Family goes there every Saturday. But I don't want to think about that. Just need some mellow music.

(LORENZO goes to his computer for music and something, maybe Annie Lennox.)

LORENZO: There we go. You want something to drink?

MAURICE: Some tap water.

LORENZO: Sure you don't want something like wine?

MAURICE: How do you have wine?

LORENZO: My mom and dad keep dozens of bottles of Manischewitz. I don't know why, maybe they think a wedding is going to break out at any moment. I siphon off a little from each and replace it with water. And I found one these computer towers in the trash that hollowed out as a secret case. And before you know it, ta-da!

(LORENZO drags an old computer tower from underneath. He removes the tower's face and takes out a bottle of wine. A piece of paper slips out and falls near the bed.)

MAURICE: What are you, a teenage James Bond?

LORENZO: Sometimes you have to practice a little bit of camouflage in life, you know? *(laughs)* Well of course you know that. But do you know your wines?

MAURICE: Kid, how old are you?

LORENZO: I'm 15. But I'll be 16 in two months. *(thinks)* God, that sounded so immature. I'm sorry.

MAURICE: You're 15?

LORENZO: Yes, why?

MAURICE: You seem, I don't know, too clever.

LORENZO: Blame the internet.

MAURICE: Yeah, I guess. Well be careful. When you're at a certain age you can know more than you should.

LORENZO: Drink?

MAURICE: No.

LORENZO: Why not?

MAURICE: Because I'm not 21 yet.

LORENZO: *(tilts bottle back and takes a gulp)* Yeah, that's rough. The disadvantage of siphoning is that you get like thirty different Manischewitz flavors crammed into one. Are you sure you never drank alcohol before?

MAURICE: Course I drank alcohol before.

LORENZO: Then why did you pretend you didn't?

MAURICE: I wasn't pretending. Just saying I shouldn't because I'm not 21 yet. I was trying to set a good example.

LORENZO: Thank you.

MAURICE: No problem. Can I have some water?

LORENZO: Coming right up.

(LORENZO exits. MAURICE begins looking around at the room.)

MAURICE: Do you have any pictures of your sister?

LORENZO: No. But why would I want a picture of my sister in my own bedroom? Kinda sick, right?

MAURICE: Maybe. So, Lorenzo-

(LORENZO comes back in with water, handing it to him.)

LORENZO: Here you go.

MAURICE: Thank you. So, Lorenzo…

LORENZO: You like saying that a lot, don't you?

MAURICE: Yes, it's catchy. So, what did your sister say about me?

LORENZO: She said that you were a total bad ass.

MAURICE: *(embarrassed giggle)* …she's got a way with words, doesn't she?

LORENZO: She's a poet.

MAURICE: You're very lucky to have such a wise sister. What else did she say?

LORENZO: That you were from St. Louis. That you left high school and joined the Marines. I read the article about you.

MAURICE: *(annoyed)* Ahh, yes. 'The' article.

LORENZO: It's a great story.

MAURICE: Yeah. They always find a way.

LORENZO: What?

MAURICE: They always find a way to tell a great story. The truth is more…nuanced. Do you know what that word means?

LORENZO: I'm 15, not retarded. FYI, I'm in AP and Honors classes.

MAURICE: Okay, my bad. An Honors student. You're like the kids I used to beat up in school. The smart ones. You're probably smarter than me.

LORENZO: Yeah. Probably. So what's it like in Afghanistan?

MAURICE: Let's not get into it.

LORENZO: But you've gotta have stories. Are we ever going to leave that place?

MAURICE: Let's just drop the war. I have two weeks back in the States and I intend to get some good food, solid sleep...

LORENZO: -Maybe a little nookie.

MAURICE: ...perhaps, yes. But not with your sister. Of course. The goal is to think as little as possible about...over there.

LORENZO: I can imagine, my Mom says we're probably going to lose the whole region.

MAURICE: We're not going to lose.

LORENZO: No offense maybe 'lose' isn't the best word. It's more...nuanced, right?

MAURICE: Exactly. Things will be better off than when we first arrived. Hopefully.

LORENZO: Even with all the religious genocide and ethnic cleansing?

MAURICE: It's not religious genocide.

LORENZO: Not anymore, they already killed everybody they wanted to. All while the US watched. Just like in Iraq.

MAURICE: I'm not going to talk to a 15-year-old kid about ethnic cleansing.

(Beat)

MAURICE: And it's not ethnic cleansing. It's neighborhood resettlement.

LORENZO: Yeah, whatever.

MAURICE: Uhhh…it's not whatever.

LORENZO: Right, I know labels are important.

MAURICE: Why did you say that?

LORENZO: I don't know. I think I heard it from my sister. Look, I'm not saying we're going to lose.

MAURICE: Good.

LORENZO: I think both sides are going to lose.

MAURICE: Both sides can't lose. Somebody has to lose and somebody has to win. Let's get back to something pleasant, like Lillian. What else did she say about me?

LORENZO: She said you were a muscular, good-looking sensitive soldier in the Army. I mean, Marines. She would always get that confused.

MAURICE: It must be contagious. I'm getting confused right now. I'd really like to see a picture of your sister.

LORENZO: I don't think I can find any. My dad doesn't like to encourage the hordes of horny teenage boys around here. Besides, who needs a picture when you can be painted with a beautiful highly-descriptive biography.

MAURICE: Why don't you take me to her room?

(MAURICE finishes water. LORENZO takes his glass and goes into the bathroom.)

LORENZO: She keeps it locked. And I don't want my dad catching you out there. Lets just sit and wait. You've gotta tell me what it's like in Kabul. I read a bunch of blogs and online papers to keep up with what's happening in Afghanistan. You're stationed on the outskirts, right?

(MAURICE finds his mailed jock strap and begins fuming.)

MAURICE: Yeah. So Lorenzo, how would you describe your sister...in your own words.

LORENZO: She is just an angel. Kind, and giving, and has...huge breast. Her face is sort of, like, um, Christmas.

MAURICE: What else about her?

LORENZO: She's just really pretty. Red bursting lips, curvaceous hips, golden hair, green eyes, like pine trees or...

MAURICE: -an emerald.

LORENZO: Right.

MAURICE: Wow, she describes herself with a lot of the same words that you use.

LORENZO: Great minds think alike.

MAURICE: Sometimes they're so great they're the same.

LORENZO: Well, yes. We are very close.

MAURICE: Lorenzo, could you come out here for a second?

(LORENZO enters and MAURICE holds up his jock strap.)

MAURICE: What is this?

LORENZO: Um…I know you're probably thinking to yourself what is your jockstrap doing here?

MAURICE: My jockstrap? How did you know it was mine?

LORENZO: My sister told me. Of course. You're probably wondering what I'm doing with that and I can explain. I took it from her room. I thought some jock left it behind and I didn't want my Dad finding it. But then she told me about you and I figured I'd keep it safely here.

(MAURICE grabs LORENZO and slams him into the bed.)

LORENZO: Okay, okay, okay. Let's calm down.

MAURICE: I'm going to pound your fucking face in.

LORENZO: No, wait…

MAURICE: Tell me the truth about Lillian, you fucking punk.

LORENZO: This is all a, a misunderstanding and… *(MAURICE raises his fist to strike him)* …WAIT, wait. Okay. I'm sorry. the truth about Lillian is… you're looking at her.

MAURICE: What the hell are you talking about?

LORENZO: I am her.

MAURICE: No, no, no. You're joking. This is a joke, right. There's a candid camera around here somewhere. And Lillian is...

LORENZO: Yes.

MAURICE: You're not serious. I mean, why would anyone do that?

LORENZO: Don't know.

MAURICE: You wouldn't do that, right? Not to me.

LORENZO: I didn't think you'd ever show up looking for her.

(MAURICE releases LORENZO.)

MAURICE: That is so fucking twisted...aaahhh!

LORENZO: Shhh, my parents.

MAURICE: Kid, you got problems.

LORENZO: I know.

MAURICE: Pretending to be a woman...

LORENZO: I didn't mean to.

MAURICE: What are you talking about? You accidentally went along with this for months. You just happen to take on the name Lillian, signed letters and emails with it.

LORENZO: You assumed I was a woman and I went along with it.

MAURICE: Why?

LORENZO: I don't know. You sounded interested in me.

MAURICE: I was interested in Lillian.

LORENZO: Well I am sort of...Lillian.

MAURICE: You are a not an barely legal hot cheerleader. You are a 15-year-old boy with too much time on his hands. The letters, cookies, e-mails, panties. The panties! Are these your panties?

LORENZO: No, usually I go commando.

MAURICE: Aww, TMI.

LORENZO: I stole those from a store.

MAURICE: How come they smell the way they do?

LORENZO: I rubbed them with a little canned tuna and hot sauce.

MAURICE: That is so fucking sick.

LORENZO: I saw how to do it on REALSEX HBO. It was a mail order company in Poughkeepsie that sends used panties to men. It's how they give fresh panties that worn smell.

(LORENZO picks up jock strap from the floor.)

LORENZO: What about your jock strap?

MAURICE: I'm not a liar. I wore it.

LORENZO: Yeah, I can smell you. Even left some hair in the crack-

MAURICE: Gimme that!

(MAURICE walks around the room and gathers his things.)

MAURICE: And the picture?

LORENZO: J Crew holiday catalog. Face like Christmas.

MAURICE: Kid, you gotta pay. For all this sick fucking...

(MAURICE punches LORENZO, who crumples to the ground. LORENZO gathers himself.)

LORENZO: Okay. Okay. Is that my payment?

MAURICE: You think this is funny? You think you're being cute?

LORENZO: *(winces in pain)* No. Sorry.

MAURICE: ...I didn't punch you that hard.

LORENZO: Sure.

MAURICE: I barely tapped you. You're not hurt.

LORENZO: Sure, sure. I'm fine. I've been hit before. It just takes a moment. One time I met this dude and after we did it, he found out I was a dude and he started punching me in the face. He was screaming about getting AIDS and shit. I thought he was going to kill me, said he was going to cut my throat and he ran back to his car. I didn't stick around because...

MAURICE: ...don't you ever shut up?

LORENZO: Sorry. Nervous habit.

(Beat)

LORENZO: Are you grossed out because I like you?

MAURICE: You don't like me. You don't know me.

LORENZO: Just so you know... I wish I was Lillian. If it makes you feel any better I wish I could be her.

MAURICE: Yeah, so wouldn't get your ass kicked.

LORENZO: No. I wish I was Lillian so you would stay. I can't do anything about my age or what I am. Isn't this what you were looking for?

MAURICE: Uh...no.

LORENZO: No family, no friends, You said you had nothing.

MAURICE: That doesn't mean I'm gay.

LORENZO: It's not about that.

MAURICE: Actually, I think it is.

LORENZO: It's about a connection, right? How many times did we fuck over email?

MAURICE: Oh god.

LORENZO: Or IM? That's all it is. An instant connection through wires, cables, and satellites. But now you're here. Now we're standing in the same room. And I feel like we know each other. I've laughed with you, I've worried about you. I've lived with you. And I even baked you fucking cookies!

(Beat)

LORENZO: I like you.

MAURICE: Kid, I don't care if you like fisting frozen turkeys while getting spanked with a rolled up newspaper.

LORENZO: Huh?

MAURICE: It's a figure of speech.

LORENZO: Where?

MAURICE: In my head, okay. The point is that I don't care what you like. You lied.

LORENZO: I'm sorry.

MAURICE: Sorry isn't good enough. You gotta pay.

LORENZO: How much was the bus ticket?

MAURICE: Not that kind of pay.

(Beat)

MAURICE: It was $55 but I'm talking about pay as in suffering. Penance.

LORENZO: Penance?

MAURICE: It's a Catholic thing.

LORENZO: You can do whatever Catholic thing you want to me.

MAURICE: Oh, really? Whatever I want?

LORENZO: Yes.

MAURICE: So I could...shove you *(backs him up)*.

LORENZO: I'd let you. You could do whatever you to me.

MAURICE: Oh, really? Whatever I want.

LORENZO: Yes.

MAURICE: *(hitting him)* And if started hitting you, then you'd be fine?

LORENZO: Yes, if you want to.

MAURICE: Why aren't you fighting back?

LORENZO: You want me to fight you?

MAURICE: Yeah. It makes it harder to kick your ass when you don't fight.

LORENZO: But I don't want to fight you, Maurice. Look, if it's sex I know a girl at school who's a total slut.

MAURICE: It's not the sex. It's the time and energy and effort. After all I've done. Months! MONTHS!

LORENZO: Maurice, my Dad might hear you.

MAURICE: You've taken months from me. Of my time, of my money, of my mind. Months you've wasted and... *(Maurice takes a moment.)* I'm telling your Dad. He'll punish you. My dad would kick my ass when I was young. Sometimes for doing nothing. It's good for you. Makes you learn things. Things you don't wanna take to. Like not lying.

LORENZO: How are you going to tell them?

MAURICE: I'm going to march in there... *(thinks)* ... okay, that's a problem.

LORENZO: My mom won't care much. She never does. But my dad might call the police. He also has a gun in his room.

MAURICE: You are going to march in there and introduce me.

LORENZO: As what, a friend?

MAURICE: As...as...I don't care. Just get in there.

LORENZO: I... don't want to.

MAURICE: Excuse me?

LORENZO: I don't want to do it.

MAURICE: I know you don't want to do it. That's why it's called punishment. Because you do something you'd rather not. I'm ordering you to get in there.

LORENZO: I'm not good with following orders.

(LORENZO and MAURICE look at each other. MAURICE moves toward him and LORENZO backs up.)

MAURICE: Lorenzo, this is stupid. Stop moving away.

LORENZO: Then stop following me.

MAURICE: Lorenzo. I'm not going to chase you.

(Beat)

(MAURICE chases LORENZO. Lorenzo throws clothes at him as obstacles. It is a silent and stealthily Maurice eventually catches him and slams Lorenzo against the wall.)

MAURICE: Now, listen up Lorenzo...

LORENZO: -Don't make me tell him.

MAURICE: You are going to learn responsibility.

LORENZO: Maurice, I don't want to be thrown from a window.

MAURICE: What?

LORENZO: He said he would throw me from a window.

MAURICE: Who?

LORENZ: My dad. Next time he caught me with a guy.

MAURICE: Well he's not catching you like that, because we didn't do anything.

LORENZO: Listen, I'm sorry for what I did, but my Dad doesn't joke around. He's a big believer in punishment.

MAURICE: So was mine. Big deal.

LORENZO: With paddles, pipes, and chains

MAURICE: What?

LORENZO: A few months ago the manager at the Greyhound station called him. Said I was loitering around the bathroom, making travelers nervous. But I was just, I don't know, hanging out. But he came. Straight from work he marched down to that station. Smiled, nodded his head, talked real nice and calm to the manager and thanked him for looking out for me. And he drove mc home in the rain and calmly told me the next time he embarrassed him like that he would throw me out of a window. Didn't know if he was serious or not. But when I was walking up the steps to the front door and he knocked me down and threw a sheet over me. He started waling on me with these chains, from the snow tires. Got a couple of good ones in on my back and stomach and there's no sign of the chains because of the sheets. And he starts kicking and cussing and spitting on me. His fucking faggot son. I stole a fishing knife from the garage. I ran up to my room and I was going to wait until he was asleep. Fuck me? Fuck him! Fuck him, fuck all these goddamn assholes! Fuck the Greyhound manager, fuck the married businessmen jerking off in the bus stop bathroom. Fuck it all. Then I thought about what you said when we got in that fight: 'why not just kill yourself?'

MAURICE: I didn't mean it like that.

LORENZO: But you were right. Fuck it all. Only take a few cuts and I'd be done. And then I got your IM about the sandstorms. And talking to you made things…less fucked. I didn't want to…do it. Maurice, you're the only one I'd let hit me, touch me, do whatever. But not him. If you make me go into that room, I'll do what I started. I'll fucking kill him and I'm not joking. And then I can slash my own throat and be happy just knowing that fucker is dead. Because I'd rather kill him, my mom, this whole fucking town, and me than let him throw me out a window. And if you make me go in there, I will.

(LORENZO dashes into the bathroom and locks the door.)

MAURICE: Kid. Hey, you're not going to…Don't. look: it's all right. Okay…okay?

SCENE FOUR: HERO

(Sounds of Kabul: trucks, motorcycles, bikes. Maybe the sound of a call to prayer from a mosque but it shouldn't be too loud. Maurice drinks the wine and notices a letter on the floor.)

MAURICE: Dear Lillian, I can't sleep. It's too quiet and I got this buzzing in my ear. I've gotten so used to mortar and gunfire that I don't know what to do when it's silent out there in Indian country. That's what we call it out there. There's the base, a few pockets in Kabul, and there's the other 90% of Afghanistan. They keep telling us that things are getting better, we're making peace, but then another blast wall goes up. It gets quieter, markets are reopening, but no one feels safe. We're all just buzzing around, keeping ourselves busy until the next explosion. We have this Afghanistani translator, we call him Bob. That's not his name but we call him that. Bob is this smiling young Pashtun. Upbeat, nice home, cute wife, never has a complaint. Well Bob was walking toward me yesterday butchering some Beyonce song and I thought 'this is what my enemy looks like. He's Bob's age, listening to rap music, playing Xbox 360, has barely grown a moustache, and he wants to kill me. People who look just like Bob and, who knows, maybe even Bob in a year. When I look over the wire, I see new satellite dishes, antennas popping up on every roof. If it wasn't for the mountains and mosques, it could almost be St. Louis. If I get home am I going to be one of those lunatics who can't keep still, can't stop thinking, can't stop living over here?

I'm not going to be able to get rid of Indian country. I want to see you. When I get back to St. Louis you should come and see me. I'm crashing on a friend's couch, but you should still come. I can show you the Arch and the good section of St. Louis. All two blocks of it. Fuck it, we won't even go back there. Why should we? There's nothing keeping me there. It's not home, just Indian country. We'll have to make our own home. We'll go to Arizona or West Texas. Some place hot and flat. Far away from a city. Nothing will look like Abilene or St. Louis or Kabul. No cell phones or antennas, no malls or hotels. Just us. What do you think?

(MAURICE picks up the letter. LORENZO enters and snatches the letter from him.)

LORENZO: What are you doing?

MAURICE: It was by your bed. I stayed up writing that. I couldn't sleep so I just planted myself in front of a computer and started typing. To my high school geometry teacher, my ex-girlfriend, my prom date, my mom. But I only had your e-mail address. Never really paid attention to how few people I really knew.

LORENZO: It's hard to get friends to stick around.

MAURICE: Yeah, in your teens that's the way it is.

LORENZO: Does it get better?

MAURICE: No.

LORENZO: Good to know. Thanks.

MAURICE: No problem. Whatever I can do to chip in.

LORENZO: Chip in?

MAURICE: Yeah, so that you don't kill yourself. Or your Dad. You're not...you know, going to that now, are you?

LORENZO: Well I didn't have any plans this weekend.

MAURICE: Good. I should be getting back to the station.

LORENZO: Oh. When does your bus leave?

MAURICE: 10 a.m.

LORENZO: You've got time.

MAURICE: Yeah, but I want to just get my ticket.

LORENZO: And spend the night in a bus station? Come on, you've come all this way. You want some more wine?

MAURICE: No, I'm good. All those different Manischewitz mixed together is not doing good things to my stomach.

LORENZO: I can get you some cereal. To soak up the wine.

MAURICE: I'll walk it off.

LORENZO: Come on, we got all night.

MAURICE: No, I can't. I've gotta get back to St. Louis. Look, but we'll talk by e-mail.

LORENZO: Yeah, right. Maurice, you're the first person I've met who is... a hero.

MAURICE: Like Aquaman.

LORENZO: No. A real hero. The first time I read about what you did-

MAURICE: -here we go again

LORENZO: I hated you.

MAURICE: What?

LORENZO: Maurice, I hate guys like you so fucking much that it makes me wanna vomit.

MAURICE: Thanks. I hate you too.

LORENZO: But I hate guys like you because I want what you got. That *(starting to swagger)* ...you know, stuff. The total bass ass hero vibe.

MAURICE: You have nothing to be jealous of.

LORENZO: Maurice, I'm a horny lil' fag in the middle of Kansas. I have plenty to be jealous of. I try to, you know, butch up. But it's like holding my breath. And then I see all those fat, saggy jowled prisses. Those old queens. Lonely, sad, wrinkled freaks wearing penny loafers. And I realize that's what I'm going to become. But I don't want to be some faggy high school drama teacher.

MAURICE: Then don't be. Be a faggy English teacher or math teacher.

LORENZO: You're so sweet.

MAURICE: Well what do you want from me? Do you want me to kiss you and make it all better?

LORENZO: Hmmm...

MAURICE: Kid, I've been really patient with you. But right now I got a dull wine headache, a destroyed image of the woman I loved, and a pair of blueballs. So I'm going to leave out that window and get back on that Greyhound back to St. Louis, make up some bullshit story about banging some bitch so I don't look like a complete idiot to my friend and then fall asleep for two days on his mom's futon.

LORENZO: But…you told me you'd be my hero.

MAURICE: I never said that.

LORENZO: Yeah you did. In September over IM.

MAURICE: Are you like my Xerox machine? How can you even remember what I said over IM?

LORENZO: I printed it out.

MAURICE: ...what?

LORENZO: I printed out your e-mails and our chats.

MAURICE: Why would you do that?

LORENZO: My parents check my computer. So I have to print out the private stuff I want to keep and delete the files.

MAURICE: And you threw these papers away?

LORENZO: No, I still have them.

MAURICE: You still have them where?

LORENZO: In my room.

MAURICE: What? You're not serious.

LORENZO: Why wouldn't I be?

MAURICE: We had cybersex over IM.

LORENZO: I read those the most.

MAURICE: Fine, but if somebody does find these papers or your mom finds them while cleaning, that's my ass. I could go to jail.

LORENZO: I keep them in a safe space.

MAURICE: Where?

LORENZO: Well it wouldn't be that safe if I told you.

MAURICE: ...Lorenzo...buddy. You wouldn't want me to get in trouble, would you?

LORENZO: Nothing is going to happen to you. Nothing ever happens to guys like you.

MAURICE: Let's work something out here.

LORENZO: Maurice, don't you have a bus to catch?

MAURICE: It can wait.

LORENZO: I thought you had to rush off. I mean, the bus is leaving in about 8 hours. Wouldn't want you to miss that.

MAURICE: Lorenzo, what would it take for you to possibly, consider giving me some of those

LORENZO: -wild, angry sex.

(Beat)

MAURICE: What else would it take?

LORENZO: A handjob.

MAURICE: Let's be reasonable.

LORENZO: A hanjo' is pretty reasonable.

MAURICE: A hanjo?

LORENZO: You know, like a banjo. But a handjob.

MAURICE: You can give a hanjo to any guy!

LORENZO: I don't want any guy! I want you.

MAURICE: Why?

(Beat)

MAURICE: Oh, you think I'm some hero. You think I'm this big macho guy.

LORENZO: Maurice even the paper said so.

MAURICE: That fucking newspaper is pretend.

LORENZO: So what if it is? It's not like you're a reality TV star or some worthless rich piece of shit with a camera. It's good pretend. The world is better because of it and so are you.

MAURICE: Lorenzo, if you think that story is real then you don't even know who I am.

LORENZO: Who cares who you think you are? I know what I think. Let's pretend. Isn't that love? You be the hero. I'll be Lillian, and everyone is happy.

MAURICE: Or we could stop pretending.

LORENZO: Why?

MAURICE: So you can grow up. So you'll stop worshipping me. This fucking story.

(Maurice rips up the story and throws in Lorenzo's face. Lorenzo goes to his desk and takes out another copy. Maurice lunges for it but he's drunk and Lorenzo is quicker.)

LORENZO: What are you going to do, rip up every copy I have? It's on the internet. It's already out in the world. You can't destroy it.

MAURICE: I'm getting out of here.

LORENZO: I'll email you. I'll send you presents, I'll write you letters.

MAURICE: Lorenzo-

LORENZO: Cause I know you'll read them. Cause I know you like me. Some part of you, likes me. That's why you'll read them. You can't destroy our connection.

MAURICE: I can try.

LORENZO: Why would you want to do that?

MAURICE: So you'll leave me alone. Wanna hear something?

LORENZO: No. Maybe. I don't know.

MAURICE: I was doing a few shifts. Working at a check-point for UNESCO.

LORENZO: Maurice, what are you talking about?

MAURICE: The story.

LORENZO: I know but…you're drunk. You don't really want me to leave you alone.

LORENZO: UNESCO is this organization for poor kids. They got a whole set-up in Kabul. Cars go in and cars go out. All day long. Every once in a while you get a bad driver trying to speed through the gates or someone difficult.

LORENZO: What if we turned off the lights, you closed your eyes, and we see what happens?

MAURICE: UNESCO was bringing in these giant sewage pipes to install at this elementary school. Children play in these puddles of hot liquid garbage. I mean just the nastiest fucking stuff you could think and they splash around it in like it's chocolate.

LORENZO: Where did you put the blindfold?

MAURICE: Lorenzo, would you shut the hell up for a minute?!? I'm trying to tell you something.

LORENZO: Fine.

MAURICE: *(exasperated)* ...fuck. Anyway, nobody wants to go help out. We draw and I lose so I gotta go on this trip to take the pipes from the airport and escort UNESCO to this school. Big philanthropy project, camera men, reporters, everyone's on board to watch what a great, kind thing we're about to do. Our job is to just escort the convoy through a rough section of 10 blocks, and get the stuff there. When he hit the bad area the trucks in front are kicking up dust so you can't even see five feet in front of your face. And that's when the shooting started. Peppering the jeep and trucks, then it starts coming on heavier. From all angles. And we're firing out of the jeep in every direction while speeding through the patch at 100. An IED explodes and the Hummer next to us goes up in a fireball. And we're firing and firing and firing. We got a few more blocks to go. I look up and can see above the smoke. On the roofs are these little kids with buckets. And they're dumping raw sewage back down on to our convoy. The same stuff we're trying to get cleaned up and put in these pipes they're hurling at us. Diapers, and cereal boxes, and oil get dumped on top of us for fun. And everybody just having a fucking blast. And one of these girls –she's wearing these neon green socks and shoes so she stuck out- she's dumping buckets of shit on us and laughing. I start firing at the roofs. I'm sure I hit a few. We clear the bad area and the shooting dies down. We get to the elementary school. We scramble out and take our positions. Two men got their heads blown off and three are AVAC'ed out.

LORENZO: What's AVAC? *(MAURICE shoots him a look)* Sorry.

MAURICE: Air Evacuation. To a hospital. In less than a minute I got two dead bodies, one guy who has an eyeball full of shrapnel, another whose right arm is hanging by a thread for these pipes. But whatever, UNESCO doesn't care. They just think it's so wonderful that we got these fucking pipes to the school. It's all a part of the progress to help these ungrateful goatfuckers since we invaded their country, right? When they take out these pipes, they can't hold water. They were shot up with holes and cracked from the ride. Who knows, maybe they were busted to begin with. But I just drove through hell for these pipes. So the UNESCO guy, some office prick with a title and badge, starts telling me there some more pipes back at the airport and everything we'll be fine if we just turn around and go back through hell again and get those pipes. I'm like 'fuck you and fuck this.' I go for a walk. Before anybody has a chance to react I've opened up some distance between me and this UN guy. I get lost in these little narrow streets. And I find this cool and quiet hidden path. At the end is this woman. She's washing clothes in a plastic bucket and hanging them up on a line. She stands up and stares at me. I sling my automatic around my shoulders and draw my handgun.

LORENZO: What?

MAURICE: It's easier to shoot somebody in close range.

LORENZO: You were going to kill her.

MAURICE: In war people get shot.

LORENZO: You guys have a code of conduct. Maurice, you're not like that. You weren't going to shoot her!

MAURICE: You don't know me.

LORENZO: But you need reasons to shoot.

MAURICE: Fuck your reasons. You want me to blame my parents? Or my Daddy hit me? Isn't that a reason? Maybe I'm sick of seeing my friends lose their arms and legs because some kid pushes a button on a remote. Maybe I'm pissed off at UNESCO, the Marine Corp, Afghanistan, those fucking flag-waving bastards who shipped us over and forgot about us. How many reasons do you need to kill?

LORENZO: I don't know.

MAURICE: Then shut up. I spin her around and I press my berretta to the back of her skull and I'm going to do this. And I'm thinking 'holy mother of fucking Jesus, I'm going to do this.'

LORENZO: Maurice

MAURICE: What? Feeling sick? Good. That's the feeling you should have when you're about to... look, then the adrenaline kicks in. And I start to feel it. I release the safety and close my eyes. And then something

70

shoots by me. I look down and it's a girl. The same girl on the roof with green socks. The one who was throwing shit at me. The one who was laughing and smiling. She's wrapped around her mother. I try to rip her off but she's glued tight. By this time the UNESCO guy and his entourage had caught up with me. One of the embedded photographers finds us yelling and screaming at each other with this mother and daughter cowering in the corner. He knew something bad was happening and he just looked at me and said, "come here and let me take your picture. Hero." And then his camera starts going off and I find myself smiling and being told to put my arms around the little girl and her mother. After a few pictures, the mother grabber her clothes, her daughter and sprinted away as quickly as possible. And that's when the UNESCO guy opened his mouth, spinning out this story. Details get added. The gunmen turned into a kidnapper with a gun. Photographer knew we were full of shit but he had to make deadline. Details get back to the Marines. Armed Service Information gets involved and the story spins faster and faster until I don't even recognize myself in it. And people play along. And I did too.

(Beat)

MAURICE: Every time I hear that hero story mentioned…it makes me want to fucking vomit. Every time I get it out of my mind and I have a few minutes of peace, somebody has to bring it right back. And then my mind start racing and I can't stop it and I can't stand it.

(MAURICE picks up the bottle and drinks the rest of the wine.)

LORENZO: So you're a liar?

MAURICE: And a coward. And an idiot. Not a hero.

(LORENZO tries to kiss him and Maurice holds him back.)

MAURICE: What are you doing?

LORENZO: You're just like me. Come on. We're here, right now. Just us. What do you want? Pretend I'm Lillian, whatever you want.

MAURICE: I don't want anything from you.

LORENZO: Maurice, you came all this way, right? You lied, I lied, we're here. You're just like me.

MAURICE: I am not.

LORENZO: Yeah, you're just like me. You're scared. You're a liar. Just like me. They push us around, fucked us over, no one cares about us. No one cares about you. I'm not even that scared of you anymore.

MAURICE: Fuck you, Lorenzo.

LORENZO: Come on, you fucking coward. You're just like me. Just like me in every way

(MAURICE shoves his hand over Lorenzo's mouth and slams him against the bed. MAURICE rips Lorenzo's shirt open.)

LORENZO: I'm sorry …wait…

MAURICE Shut up.

(MAURICE presses his fist down hard into him. LIGHTS GO OUT.)

SCENE FIVE: MORNING CALM

(It's morning and still. There's a tangle of sheets, arms and feet on the bed. MAURICE moans and rolls over on to LORENZO. Smothered under the bigger body, LORENZO reaches for his watch. He looks at it and panics. He tries to get out, but MAURICE won't move. After struggling against the dead weight, LORENZO manages to slip out underneath. He looks around the bed and on the floor for his pajamas and finds Maurice's underwear. Quickly slipping it on and oblivious to the fact that the shorts are slipping off his waist, LORENZO runs out of the room. Moments later, he returns with a cordless phone in one hand while he holds his shorts with the other.)

LORENZO: Mom? Sorry, I know I'm only supposed to call in case of emergencies, but where are you?...Okay, how come nobody woke me up?...NO, no. I was just curious. All right, bye. Wait...when will you be home? Okay...bye.

(LORENZO looks around in a daze. He drops the phone and walks back out. MAURICE wakes up, rubs his head and remembers where he is and what happened. Unable to find his underwear, MAURICE covers himself in the sheets and sits up in bed. LORENZO enters with two hardboiled eggs.)

LORENZO: My mom left this for us...well for me. But...

(LORENZO throws one egg to MAURICE.)

MAURICE: I gotta get out of here.

LORENZO: It's 10. I guess you missed your bus.

MAURICE: There's another one in the afternoon. You folks still here?

LORENZO: Nope. Ham & Eggery. Just something my family does on the weekend.

MAURICE: Tradition.

LORENZO: Yeah.

MAURICE: Deep.

LORENZO: It's the Ham & Eggery.

MAURICE: Why didn't they get you?

LORENZO: My dad couldn't sleep so he was up all night.

MAURICE: What?

LORENZO: But he was downstairs. Watching TV. He didn't want to wait for me, so they just went and left me behind.

MAURICE: So we're safe?

LORENZO: For now.

MAURICE: So I can scream at the top of my lungs?

LORENZO: Sure, if you want to.

MAURICE: Cool.

LORENZO: Well?

MAURICE: *(quietly)* Ahhhh.

LORENZO: We can do whatever we want...for a half-hour at least.

(LORENZO gets close to kiss him. MAURICE pulls away.)

MAURICE: You should have some salt on your egg.

(LORENZO walks into the bathroom.)

MAURICE: You keep salt in the bathroom?

LORENZO: Bootleg facial scrub. Sea salt gets rid of the acne.

MAURICE: Where are my shorts?

LORENZO: What?

MAURICE: My underwear.

LORENZO: Oh. I guess I'm wearing it. Sorry. I'm so used to going without it, I couldn't tell if it was yours or just an old pair of mine laying around that had been stretched.

MAURICE: Well can I have it?

LORENZO: *(O/S)* Salt or shorts? Which one do you want first?

MAURICE: Shorts, please.

(MAURICE tosses the pajamas into the bathroom. LORENZO tosses out the shorts. MAURICE changes and LORENZO comes back out in his pajamas and eating his egg. MAURICE puts on his pants and shirt.)

MAURICE: Could I have the letters?

LORENZO: Maurice…

MAURICE: so that I can sleep at night not worrying about being thrown in jail.

(LORENZO removes a shoe box from the computer tower. He pulls the letters out. MAURICE grabs them all in his hand.)

LORENZO: What are you doing?

MAURICE: Taking the letters.

LORENZO: Not all of them. Just the dirty ones. *(LORENZO sorts and picks out a dozen or so letters.)* These.

MAURICE: Lorenzo, how do I know there's not more dirty letters laying around?

LORENZO: Those are the ones.

MAURICE: I can't risk my safety on the chance of a couple of extra letters being left behind. You might as well hand over the rest.

LORENZO: Why won't you let me keep something?

MAURICE: Because they're not yours! It's my words. My letters. They weren't even written for you! Personal stuff is in there.

LORENZO: That's what I love about them. They remind me of you.

MAURICE: Why do you need a reminder for? I'm here!

LORENZO: But you're going! So I'm keeping them.

MAURICE: Fine.

LORENZO: Fine.

(MAURICE grabs the letters. LORENZO puts the rest back in the sneaker box, crams it into the computer tower, and slides it back under the bed. Maurice dresses.)

MAURICE: Great.

LORENZO: Look, Maurice I'm sorry.

MAURICE: Thanks for breakfast.

LORENZO: I hope you're not freaking out about what we…thank you.

(Beat)

LORENZO: Can I e-mail you?

MAURICE: You can do whatever you want.

LORENZO: What I meant is will you write back?

MAURICE: If I have a good internet connection, who knows. They're moving us around a lot.

LORENZO: Then I can send you some letters, or care packages with some food and you'll get them?

MAURICE: I'll try. But I might be busy getting shot at.

LORENZO: Don't say that, ok? *(Pause)* Thank you.

(LORENZO goes in for a goodbye kiss. MAURICE tries a friendly hug. They both settle on a handshake.)

LORENZO: Wow, a handshake.

MAURICE: Nothing wrong with a handshake Goodbye... and Lorenzo?

LORENZO: What?

MAURICE: Get off the internet.

LORENZO: Why?

MAURICE: Because there's a million and one things to do besides looking for sex and reading bullshit blogs.

LORENZO: Online I can check pictures, profiles, if someone harasses me I can block them out. The internet
isn't that bad.

MAURICE: I promise you: the real world is a lot better.

LORENZO: But then who's going to block the bad stuff?

MAURICE: I don't know. You just get out there into the
world. If you need advice, you can write me…if you
want?

LORENZO: Really?

MAURICE: Sure. Just nothing dirty.

LORENZO: I promise.

MAURICE: Well…goodbye.

LORENZO: Wait! Let me get you some food for the road.

MAURICE: Lorenzo. The egg is fine.

LORENZO: But you might want a snack or something.

(LORENZO exits to the pantry.)

LORENZO: *(O/S)* Oh, I know: my mom has this stash of
granola in the towel closet.

MAURICE: What? Why?

LORENZO: *(O/S)* She likes to hide food around the house. We pretend not to notice. Cookies, pretzels, candy are everywhere. One time I found some bottles of chocolate milk floating in the tank of her toilet. But she has this organic, holistic, no-preservatives granola in the closet. I think it's her attempt to be healthy. Whenever my mom is feeling guilty about eating badly, she just takes fistfuls of granola and crams them into her mouth. I tried to tell her granola actually has a lot of fat in it. And even if it is good for you, when you eat at Ham & Eggery all the time that pretty much cancels out any health benefits. I read this study online about fatty triglyceride acids that says I'm right.

MAURICE: You're a very smart kid. You just need to let the internet go. Stop using it and people as a crutch.

(MAURICE reaches underneath the bed and opens the box of letters.)

LORENZO: *(O/S)* I'll try. Maurice, I know you don't want to hear this, but I'm going to miss you. And I'm going to change for you.

(MAURICE puts the rest of the letters in his jacket. Then he slides the computer back under the bed. He exits out the window.)

LORENZO: *(O/S)* And I think it's because…I love you. There, I couldn't say it to your face. I didn't want you laughing or yelling at me. So I'm screaming it from the other side of the house, I love you. I love you in the other room. I love you in the same room. I love you over in Afghanistan. I love you when you're in the Green Zone. I love you when you're scared, when you're hungry, when you're cold. And when you think you're going to die, then I feel like I am too, because I love you, love you, love-

(LORENZO enters with bags of granola and dried fruit.)

SCENE SIX: CARE PACKAGE

(LORENZO chomps on some snacks as he writes. He garbles his words through a mush of granola and fruit.)

LORENZO: Dear Maurice, It's LL here. Again. Just in case my other emails got lost in cyberspace or never made it to you...I figured it couldn't hurt to follow up. I was just e-mailing you to see if you got that care package I sent you with granola and fruit? I'm eating some of the leftover stash. You mentioned that you were moving around a lot so it might have fallen into the wrong hands. How are you doing? Get back to me when you can. Lov- *(thinks)* Sincerely...Respectfully, LL.

(LORENZO slaps himself as he remembers...)

LORENZO: Dear Maurice, sorry. I know I just sent you an email but I forgot to ask if you didn't receive the package, then send me your new address and I can ship over another one. Wondering how you're doing or what's the weather like over there? It's starting to get cold here. 'Prairie cold' as my dad likes to say. I read that mountains can sometimes block vector winds. But I guess when you're that high up it doesn't matter. Okay, I'm going to stop writing now. Going to go out and meet some people as you suggested. Not online. You'll be happy to know that I haven't even gone into chat rooms or anything in a month. I haven't even looked at our letters. I've been trying to change. So there's this group for teens 'questioning their sexuality' that I was a part of but I never went to any of the meetings because it was lame. Then the school board cancelled our funding and so we don't have to pretend any more. Now we're just 'gay teens' and it's cool. We've become like this rebel group, meeting in secret places, trying not to get busted, e-mailing in code in case our parents break into our computers. A lot of secret spy stuff. Everybody wants to know who's apart of the group but we try to stay one step ahead. We never meet in the same place twice. Some of the guys are all right, but I don't want to be seen with the flamers, because then that would be, like, announcing 'it'. I have it rough at school but the flamers get beaten up all the time. There's one boy I'm interested in and I think he likes me too. But he's a flamer. If he even came within a mile of my house my Dad would kill me. At school we can only exchange looks in the hallway. I guess I'm still not brave enough. Okay. Going to get off the internet now, I swear. Closing down the windows. signing off email, logging off the computer.

(Beat)

LORENZO: You know it's my birthday soon. Just letting you know. If you were curious or, wanted to…I don't know. Anyway, logging off, logging off and getting out. I'll talk to you soon. Seeya. Bye. Bye…

(LORENZO opens his mouth but stops himself from speaking again and exits. MAURICE comes out. He's back in Kabul and reading the letter. He tries to start writing but can't.)

MAURICE: Dear LL, On the way back home from Abilene, something very strange happened...oh, I know it's been awhile... *(starts again)* Greetings, I was busy. I'm a busy busy person and days just seem to fade into weeks and then months, before you know it letters have been sitting unanswered. But I have something exciting to tell you... Lorenzo...

(MAURICE tries to sound esteemed. LORENZO enters, reading the letter and drinking Manischewitz.)

MAURICE: Over the course of a man's life, one learns certain facts about oneself *(to himself)* Oneself?

LORENZO: Who the hell says 'oneself'? Maurice you're not sounding like yourself.

MAURICE: In due time I will be able to tell you the facts I have learned about myself. For now, please accept my best wishes and hopes as a sign that I still...care for your well-being. Respectfully, Sgt. Maurice A. Creely.

(MAURICE exits. LORENZO finishes reading the letter. Then he rolls to the floor and reaches under the bed for the computer tower. He takes out the box and is about to file the letter when he lifts it up and instantly knows something is wrong. He tosses away the lid and sees all the letters are gone. He starts to panic.)

LORENZO: Mom?!? Dad?!?

(LORENZO races out of the room. He runs back in. His eyes look around for possible places he misplaced the letters. He rummages through his desk and yanks out the drawer, dumping everything on the floor. He ransacks his room, clothes, bed sheets, papers get tossed around. He runs into the bathroom and destroys that too. Finally he collapses in the bathroom, heaving for breath. MAURICE enters wearing Marine parade dress.)

MAURICE: Dear Lorenzo, You didn't respond to my last letter. I have a feeling why. And you haven't been responding to my e-mails the past few weeks. I hope you're doing well. I'm back in the States for two weeks. I'm also getting married. I met the best lady on my last leave. On my way home from Abilene in fact. That's what I was trying to tell you. It was good luck, or fate. We ended up talking on the bus all the way back and I stayed in contact with her for months over the internet. Some of her family thinks it's a little rushed, but I laid on some of your lines to them: 'what are you so afraid of?' Okay, I said more than that but you get the point. We're doing it at her church. I'm nervous because I haven't been to church in years. I keep thinking I'm going to walk in the front door and struck down by lightning. Her name is Lenore. I couldn't find a Lillian. But I found something close. I hope. We're going to have just enough time for the honeymoon before I have to shipped back for one last tour of duty. Then I plan on moving somewhere, going to night school and starting a family. Maybe Arizona. I started reflecting on the things I've done in my life and, of course, you came up. And our letters. I wanted to apologize to you for…

well you know what I did. To make it up to you, I've enclosed something to remember me by.

(LORENZO walks out with scrapbook. He opens it and finds all their letters.)

MAURICE: The way you were keeping the letters was disgusting. Not a good way to store something. Especially if you want it to last. You'll find all the letters and emails. I even rewrote the ones where I misspelled the cuss words. But they're all there, with their original meaning intact.

LORENZO: I appreciate...Maurice, I...

MAURICE: Lorenzo, I think you're the best person I know...after Lenore. Okay, maybe you're tied with her.

LORENZO: Maurice...

MAURICE: Stay safe and keep dodging all those people trying to hurt you or take advantage of you. It's Indian country everywhere these days, so you have to be safe. Please be safe.

LORENZO I love you.

MAURICE: Morning is breaking here. And by tonight I'll be a married man. And by next week I'll be back in Indian country, so it's a crap shoot whether I'll make it or not.

LORENZO: I love you.

MAURICE: But if you don't hear from me again, I just wanted to tell you...

LORENZO: I love you.

MAURICE: In case I never see you again...I wish you all the best...

LORENZO: I love you.

MAURICE: And I...love you.

LORENZO: Thank you.

MAURICE: I can't believe I almost went my whole life with this fist pressed against my chest. Then I stopped listening to all those voices, let myself be... loved. If I make it back home, I know I can have a life. The problem is now I'm really scared. Now that I have Lenore, I'm so terrified of losing what I just found.

LORENZO: Maurice. Stay safe.

MAURICE: That's all I can try to do. Well, signing off here. Sincerely. And with love.

LORENZO: Always.

THE END

More Great Plays From
Original Works Publishing

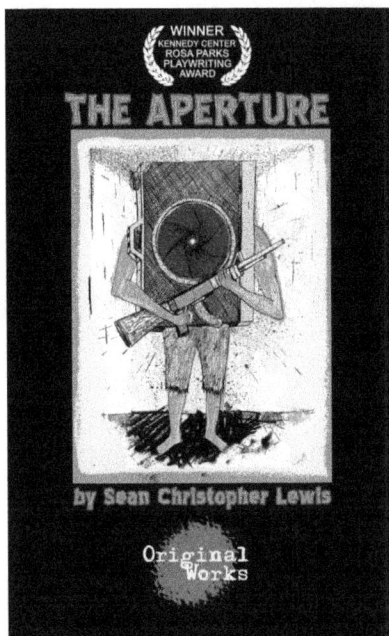

The Aperture by Sean Christopher Lewis

Synopsis: *The Aperture* takes audiences on a wild journey that explores America's fetishizing of global turbulence, violence and race. Halfway between dream and reality the piece explores the relationship of an American artist trying to save a boy soldier from Uganda.

Cast Size: 1 Male, 1 Female (playing multiple roles)

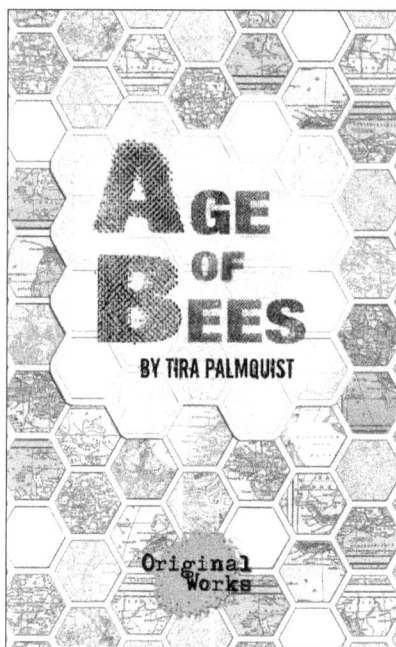

Age of Bees by Tira Palmquist

Synopsis: The bees have gone, disease and scarcity are rampant, but Mel, a young pollinator, finds refuge on an isolated farm. This place is fertile and safe, and Mel counts herself lucky to have a place where – even if it is not exactly happy – she has a purpose. When that purpose and safety are threatened, Mel faces an awful choice: will she risk leaving this relative safety, or will she hide from greater dangers, even if it means giving up some chance that something good can grow in this ruined world?

Cast Size: 1 Male, 3 Females

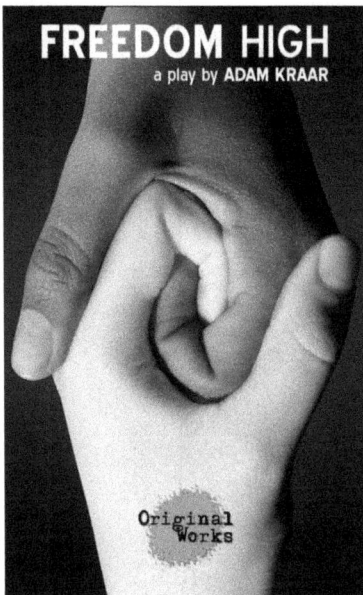

FREEDOM HIGH
a play by ADAM KRAAR

Original Works

Freedom High
by Adam Kraar

Synopsis: Inspired by actual events, FREEDOM HIGH takes place in June 1964, when black Civil Rights workers trained hundreds of white volunteers to work in Mississippi registering blacks to vote. Jessica, a young white volunteer, has no idea has no idea how dangerous – both physically and emotionally – the project will be. Instead, she throws herself into learning non-violent tactics and stubbornly trying to befriend an angry, wounded veteran of the Movement.

When three Civil Rights workers who'd been at the training the previous week disappear, the volunteers are forced to decide if they can risk their lives for a mission that seems doomed. Jessica discovers the deep – sometimes dark – complexity of her motivations, and those of everyone else involved.

Cast Size: 4 Males, 3 Females (with doubling). Up to 16 actors may be used

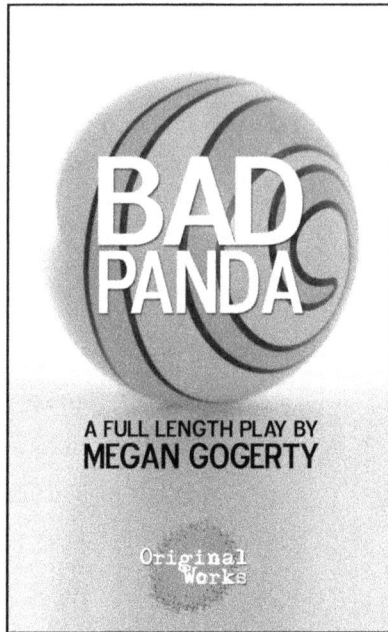

<u>Bad Panda</u> by Megan Gogerty

Synopsis: They're the last two pandas on earth. It's mating season. One of them falls in love with a crocodile. Who is gay. And then the baby comes. In this sweet celebration of non-traditional families, Gwo Gwo the panda must balance his newfound desire for Chester the crocodile with his obligations to his prescribed panda mate, Marion. The animals eat, mate, splash around in identity politics, wrestle with the ambivalence of parenthood, and love one another as only families can.

Cast Size: 2 Males, 1 Female

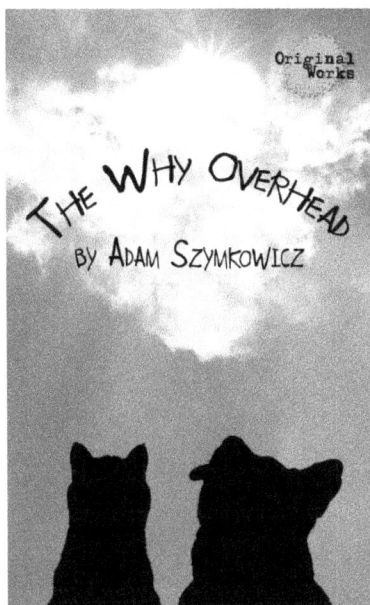

The Why Overhead
by Adam Szymkowicz

Synopsis: At the call center, all are desperate to connect with each other, seek greater meaning and take their desires to extremes. Sam is in love with Violet, a customer who called once with a warranty question, and he smashes all barriers to rendezvous with her. Alan and Sid are blinded in their rivalry for Jessica and together, build a decorative glass window over her cubicle to worship her under. Annie and Nigel have a hate-hate relationship and are each plotting the other's demise. Karen, the department head, plays hooky and makes plans with her sometimes talkative dog to leave the working world entirely in favor of the hobo life. Donald is home too, plotting revenge for being canned as office manager. In the end, the CEO, Mr. Henderson, will sweep in and make everything right, because that's what CEO's do, right?

Cast Size: 7 Males, 5 Females

<u>Nurture</u> by Johnna Adams

Synopsis: Doug and Cheryl are horrible single parents drawn together by their equally horrible daughters. The star-crossed parental units' journey from first meeting to first date, to first time, to first joint parent-teacher meeting, to proposal and more. They attempt to form a modern nuclear family while living in perpetual fear of the fruit of their loins and someone abducting young girls in their town.

Cast Size: 1 Male, 1 Female

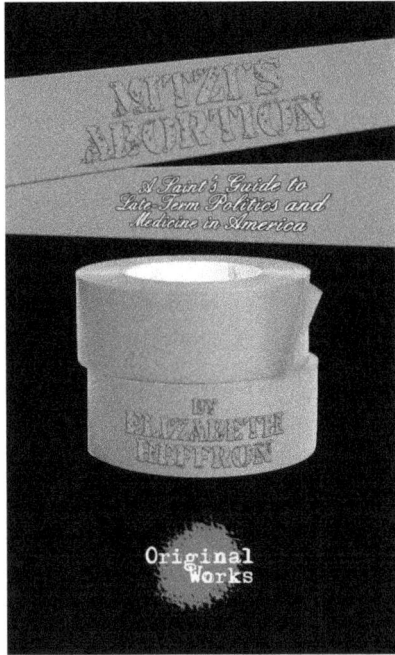

<u>Mitzi's Abortion</u> by Elizabeth Heffron

Synopsis: With humor, intelligence and honesty, Mitzi's Abortion explores the questions that have shaped the national debate over abortion, and reminds us that whatever we may think we believe, some decisions are neither easy nor simple when they become ours to make. A generous and compassionate comedy with serious themes about a young woman trying to make an intensely personal decision in a system determined to make it a political one.

Cast Size: 4 Males, 3 Female

NOTES

NOTES

NOTES

NOTES

www.ingramcontent.com/pod-product-compliance
Lightning Source LLC
Chambersburg PA
CBHW062010040426
42447CB00010B/1987